JOHN PAUL
JONES
FATHER OF THE AMERICAN NAVY

SPECIAL LIVES IN HISTORY THAT BECOME

Signature LIVES

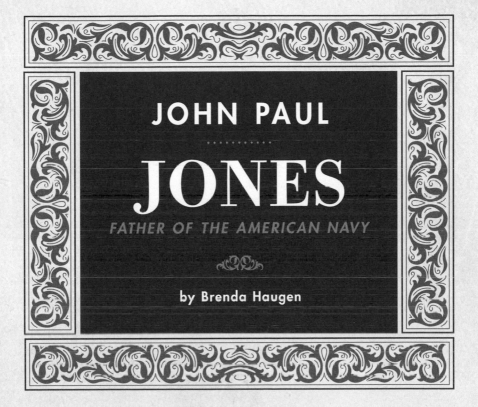

JOHN PAUL

JONES

FATHER OF THE AMERICAN NAVY

by Brenda Haugen

Content Adviser: J. Dennis Robinson,
Editor, SeacoastNH.com

Reading Adviser: Rosemary G. Palmer, Ph.D.,
Department of Literacy, College of Education,
Boise State University

COMPASS POINT BOOKS ✦ MINNEAPOLIS, MINNESOTA

Compass Point Books
3109 West 50th Street, #115
Minneapolis, MN 55410

Visit Compass Point Books on the Internet at *www.compasspointbooks.com*
or e-mail your request to *custserv@compasspointbooks.com*

Editor: Jill Kalz
Lead Designer: Jaime Martens
Photo Researcher: Svetlana Zhurkina
Page Production: The Design Lab, Bobbie Nuytten
Cartographer: XNR Productions, Inc.
Educational Consultant: Diane Smolinski

Managing Editor: Catherine Neitge
Art Director: Keith Griffin
Production Director: Keith McCormick
Creative Director: Terri Foley

*To my grandpa, John Lawrence Kingston, a U.S. Navy
veteran of World War II and my own personal hero—BH*

Library of Congress Cataloging-in-Publication Data
Haugen, Brenda.
John Paul Jones : father of the American navy / by Brenda Haugen.
p. cm. — (Signature lives)
Includes bibliographical references and index.
ISBN 0-7565-0829-0 (hardcover)
1. Jones, John Paul, 1747–1792—Juvenile literature. 2. Admirals—United
States—Biography—Juvenile literature. 3. United States. Navy—
Biography—Juvenile literature. 4. United States—History—Revolution,
1775–1783—Naval operations—Juvenile literature. I. Title II. Series.

E207.J7H26 2005
973.3'5'092—dc22   2004023133

Signature Lives

REVOLUTIONARY WAR ERA

The American Revolution created heroes—and traitors—
who shaped the birth of a new nation: the United States
of America. "Taxation without representation" was a serious
problem for the American colonies during the mid-1700s.
Great Britain imposed harsh taxes and didn't give the
colonists a voice in their own government. The colonists
rebelled and declared their independence from Britain—
the war was on.

John Paul Jones

Table of Contents

1 NOT YET BEGUN TO FIGHT

❧✕❧

With water pouring in and flames leaping from the few places that weren't wet, the *Bonhomme Richard* wouldn't stay afloat much longer. Every sailor on board could see that.

The ship flew a red, white, and blue flag representing the newly formed United States. For four years, as the Revolutionary War raged, the Continental Navy of the United States had been fighting the much larger British navy. The British had won victory after victory at sea against the Americans. Now, in 1779, it looked as though the *Bonhomme Richard* would be one more American ship captured or sunk by the British.

For more than two hours, the *Bonhomme Richard* had been locked in battle with a British

John Paul Jones's most triumphant moment came in 1779 during the battle with the British ship Serapis.

9

ship called the *Serapis*. The cannons of the *Serapis* were pounding the *Bonhomme Richard*. Cannonballs had torn open holes in the *Bonhomme Richard's* wooden sides. Below the main deck, water rushed in, filling the ship's bottom and threatening to drown the prisoners held there. When one of the ship's officers went below deck, he found the water rising almost to his chin.

Captain Jones had trained his men well in hand-to-hand combat.

On the main deck, conditions were even worse. The decks were slippery with the blood of sailors wounded or killed in battle. Fires burned in several places, and sailors rushed to put out the flames with buckets of water. If the fires spread to the magazine inside the *Bonhomme Richard*, the ship would be blown apart.

Clearly, the time had come for the *Bonhomme Richard's* captain to surrender. The two ships had sailed so close to each other during battle that sailors had lashed them together, intensifying the fighting. The British captain called out to the commander of the American ship, "Will you surrender, sir?" There would be no shame in surrendering after fighting so bravely for more than two hours. But the answer from the sinking American ship surprised him. According to legend, the captain of the *Bonhomme Richard* replied, "I have not yet begun to fight!"

The captain of the American ship was John Paul Jones. These words helped make him famous, even though his ship was lost in battle. His deeds helped him become America's first great naval hero. 🐚

> *In 2002, researchers investigated a shipwreck near Filey Bay, England, that was thought to be the* Bonhomme Richard, *sunk by the British in 1779. Its size, condition, location, and approximate age all suggested that is was indeed the* Bonhomme Richard; *however, research continues today to try to confirm the findings.*

2 DREAMS OF THE SEA

❧❦❧

John Paul Jones began his life thousands of miles from North America in a small cottage built by a wealthy landowner for his hired help. John Paul Jones was born on July 6, 1747, on a large estate called Arbigland in the town of Kirkbean, Kirkcudbright, Scotland, a part of Great Britain. His given name was John Paul. Only years later did he add the last name "Jones."

John was one of seven children born to John Paul Sr. and his wife, Jean MacDuff Paul. Two of the Paul children died while they were still infants. Young John grew up with an older brother, William; two older sisters, Elizabeth and Jane; and one younger sister, Mary Ann.

John's mother was the daughter of a farmer who

For his heroism in defending his adopted country, John Paul Jones is often called "The Father of the American Navy."

lived about six miles (10 kilometers) from Arbigland. Jean was smart and good at keeping things clean and tidy. William Craik, the owner of Arbigland, had hired her as his housekeeper.

Jean was already working at Arbigland in the 1730s when John's father was hired as head gardener of the 1,400-acre (560-hectare) estate. After seeing some of the work John Paul Sr. had done at other homes, Craik chose him to help construct the lush, fragrant gardens that would decorate Arbigland. Thanks in part to John Paul Sr.'s work, the magnificent property smelled of flowers.

Soon after the gardener and housekeeper met, they fell in love, married, and started a family.

The Pauls lived in a white stone cottage on the estate. Close to the gardens that John Paul Sr. tended, the setting could hardly have been prettier. Yet, the small home had only three or four rooms, a cramped space for a family of seven. However, the Pauls did their best to appreciate what they had. Jean kept the cottage organized and cozy.

The Pauls' cottage stood at the top of a grassy slope that led to a body of water called the Firth of watched small fishing boats and large sailing ships make their way through the Firth of Solway to the Irish Sea. On a clear day, he could see across the waterway and catch a glimpse of England.

Young John attended school in Kirkbean for sev-

The birthplace of John Paul Jones is now a museum.

eral years. The schools of Scotland in the 1700s were well respected, and many Scottish students went on to attend universities in Scotland's large cities. However, John's mind was on other things.

"I had made the art of war at sea in some degree

British and French ships battled off the coast of Spain in 1758.

my study, and had been fond of the navy from boyish days up," he later wrote in a letter.

According to one story, John liked to order his young playmates around as they paddled small rowboats around a pond. Pretending to be an admiral leading a fleet in battle, he stood above his friends on a small cliff and yelled commands to them.

It was no wonder John was "fond of the navy." The British navy was the mightiest fighting force of its time, and Great Britain (including England, Scotland, and Ireland) was known as "the ruler of the seas." When John was a boy, Great Britain fought France in the French and Indian War in North America. The two countries battled for control of territory in North America and for superiority on the seas. John grew up hearing stories of the great victories the British navy scored around the globe.

But John had little hope of becoming an officer in the British navy. Becoming an officer required friends in positions of power, and the Paul family had no such connections. Even as head gardener of a large estate, John's father was considered lower class by British society.

The best John's parents could do was to place their son as an apprentice aboard a merchant ship. In 1761, at the age of 13, John packed up his belongings and caught a ride on a small boat headed for the port at Whitehaven, England. There he boarded a merchant ship named *Friendship* for his first ocean voyage and a life on the sea. He had signed a contract to serve for seven years. Even though he would earn little money as an apprentice, he would learn all the skills needed to sail a ship.

During the 1700s, recruiters had little trouble finding young men willing to be sailors.

John also would learn how difficult life at sea could be. Sailors could be at sea for months at a time. They often ate the same food for breakfast, lunch, and dinner. Beef, dried peas, and hard biscuits made a typical meal. Fruit was rare, though by the late 1700s, British sailors would add limes to their diet to help prevent scurvy, a disease caused by a lack of vitamin C. Because crews couldn't drink the salty seawater, they brought along their own fresh-water, which didn't stay fresh for very long. After a few weeks, a film of slime covered the water, but the sailors had no choice. Their bodies needed water, so they had to drink it. They also drank a lot of alcohol.

The crew slept in hammocks hung in cramped spaces below the decks. Their bathroom was a hole in the deck of the ship. Because freshwater was strictly rationed, sailors had to use the salty seawater

John Paul Jones spent much of his life sailing along and between the Atlantic coasts.

for bathing. Many sailors didn't bother to wash. That fact, combined with the lack of proper bathrooms, made the space below the ship's deck smell horrible.

To add to their discomfort, sailors usually dressed in wool clothing. Wool kept them warm, but once it got wet, the material didn't dry easily. Sailors' clothes were almost always damp, uncomfortable, and covered with salt from the seawater.

While these conditions were bad, the work the ship's crew did made life no more pleasant. A sailing ship ran on wind power and the muscle power of its crew. Sailors pushed and pulled heavy loads around the ship. They climbed high into the rigging to position the sails to catch the wind. With the wind blowing hard and the ship rocking in the water, high-climbing sailors had to cling tightly to ropes. If they lost their grip, they might fall into the ocean or onto the deck below.

In John Paul Jones's day, few sailors could swim. If a sailor fell into the sea, he was likely to drown. Even if he could swim, the cold temperature of the ocean often claimed the man's life. The big sailing ships were difficult to steer and couldn't change course quickly enough to save a drowning or freezing sailor.

Sailing at this time in the North Atlantic Ocean was particularly dangerous because the French and Indian War continued to rage on. Although John's ship, the *Friendship*, carried a crew of only 28, the ship was equipped with 18 guns for defense and

protection. Led by Robert Benson, the *Friendship* carried everything from sugar and tobacco to iron and wood planks. The crew traveled between Great Britain, the West Indies, and the American colonies.

John was happy when the *Friendship* finally arrived in Virginia in 1761. His brother, William, had moved to Fredericksburg, Virginia, and was earning a respectable living as a tailor. When the *Friendship* docked, John got a chance to visit him. Sitting in

Sailors were often away from their loved ones for months at a time, sometimes years, so crewmates acted as a "second family" for many.

William's shop, John met some of the community's leaders. Wealthy members of Fredericksburg came to William's shop, and John enjoyed listening to these gentlemen chat about life in Virginia. In fact, John was so charmed with Virginia and its people, he promised himself that someday he would live there, too.

John spent three years as an apprentice and made eight voyages on the *Friendship*. He began to master the skills needed to navigate on the open seas. When his employer sold his ship due to hard times, he released John from his apprenticeship and allowed him to find work on his own.

John found a job aboard the *King George*, a slave-carrying ship based in Whitehaven, England. Two years later, he changed jobs and moved up to first mate on another slave ship, *Two Friends*, which was based in Kingston, Jamaica.

The *Two Friends* carried slaves from Africa to the islands of the West Indies to work on sugar plantations. Under the decks of the slave ships, people were chained together by their hands and feet and laid side by side like logs.

Slave ships were so filthy they often could be smelled from miles away. Whippings and other brutalities were common. Each morning, crews of the *Two Friends* had to remove the bodies of the slaves who had died overnight from starvation or disease.

Many scholars believe that as many as half of all slaves shipped from Africa to the West Indies died, either on the journey or once they reached the islands. Slaves started their journey in good health,

Slaves were considered cargo and kept below decks in an area called the hold.

*Sailors through-
out the 18th and
19th centuries
charted their
course using
octants and
other hand-held
navigational
tools.*

as buyers would not pay for sickly-looking workers, so the high mortality rate indicates that the slaves' treatment on board the ships was savage.

John made a great deal of money transporting slaves across the Atlantic, profiting from the misery of others for a number of years. But in 1767, he quit working on the *Two Friends*, finally sickened by the treatment of the slaves. He was offered a ride home from Jamaica to Scotland by Samuel McAdam, the Scottish captain of a ship named *John*. On the way back to Scotland, both McAdam and the first mate died, likely of malaria. Of the eight remaining sailors on board, John was the only one who knew how to navigate. He brought the *John* safely back to its home port.

A sailor could use an octant to find his position on the sea by measuring the altitude of the sun and other heavenly objects from the horizon. Readings taken on the octant and the use of a special chart pinpointed the ship's position.

The owner of the ship was so grateful that he offered command of its next voyage to John. The gardener's son who had once dreamed of commanding his own ship had become a sea captain. ❧

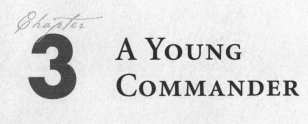

3 A YOUNG COMMANDER

❦

Although he was only 21 years old, John Paul proved to be a strict captain. He kept his ship clean and treated his crews well, but he demanded respect in return. Paul insisted that his crew work hard and follow orders. He had light brown hair and hazel eyes and stood about 5 and a half feet (165 centimeters) tall. He didn't appear imposing, yet when one of his sailors failed to follow his rules, Paul punished him.

One of the most common punishments aboard ships in the 1700s was flogging, a horribly painful ordeal involving whipping. Captains had disorderly sailors beaten with heavy whips that often left the sailors' backs bloody.

In the summer of 1770, some members of Paul's

Despite his rough life at sea, John Paul Jones was often polite, well-mannered, and flawlessly groomed.

crew tried to organize a mutiny and take control of the vessel. The ship's carpenter, Mungo Maxwell, led the unruly group.

From the beginning of the voyage, Maxwell had caused trouble for Paul. He talked back and worked only when he wanted to work. Maxwell also knew Paul's background, and he wasn't going to take orders from the son of a lowly gardener.

Maxwell had pushed Paul too far, though, and would suffer Paul's temper. After stopping the mutiny, Paul ordered Maxwell flogged as punishment for his disloyalty. Maxwell was tied to the ship by his wrists with his back exposed and flogged a dozen times.

When the *John* arrived at its next stop, an island in the West Indies called Tobago, Maxwell immediately took action. He sued Paul for the flogging he had received. Maxwell would get no satisfaction, though. Paul testified that Maxwell was disobedient and didn't do his work. The court threw out

Maxwell's case, saying that his wounds wouldn't kill him, and that he had earned the beating through his own bad behavior.

The tropical island of Tobago lies in the southeastern West Indies.

29

Enraged, Maxwell quit the *John* and sailed back to Scotland aboard the *Barcelona Packet*. Paul was glad to be rid of Maxwell, but this wasn't the last he would hear of him.

On the way back to Scotland, Maxwell developed a fever and died. Maxwell's father insisted his son's death was the result of the flogging. When Paul arrived back in Scotland, he was arrested and thrown in jail.

After a few days, Paul got out of jail on bail and immediately set out to collect evidence to prove his innocence. He traveled back to the West Indies to get documents from the trial involving Maxwell and secured a statement from the captain of the *Barcelona Packet*, James Eastment. Captain Eastment backed Paul's side of the story, saying Maxwell had been perfectly healthy when he boarded the *Barcelona Packet*. According to Eastment, Maxwell became ill during the voyage back to Scotland.

Paul quickly was cleared of being responsible for Maxwell's death. It was not the only time Captain Paul would have to deal with a mutiny, however.

While Paul was dealing with his legal problems, the *John* was sold. Again he was without a job—but not for long. In October 1772, he was hired to command a larger British merchant ship called the *Betsy*. As the ship's captain, Paul didn't just earn a flat fee for his work. He shared in the profits his voyages made for the ship's owner. Paul soon earned enough money to begin planning for his retirement—and that home in Virginia he had been dreaming about since visiting his brother.

On his second voyage aboard the *Betsy*, however, Paul encountered trouble. The ship needed repairs before the trip to Tobago could begin. While waiting for the repairs to be finished, Paul became ill. More than two weeks passed before he felt well enough to sail again. While he was regaining his strength, much of the *Betsy's* cargo spoiled. There would be no profits if he had nothing to sell.

The West Indies is a collection of islands that lies between North America and South America.

The cargo did include some wine, which could still be sold, so the *Betsy* sailed to the West Indies. Once there, the crew expected to be paid. It was just before Christmas, and many of the crew members wanted to celebrate the holiday with friends and family living in Tobago.

Paul had other plans, though. Due to costly repairs to the ship and the loss of part of the cargo, Paul decided to pay his crew when they returned to London rather than now. He'd reinvest what money he had in new cargo to take back to England and pay the crew with the profits.

The sailors were not pleased, and some began to complain. One sailor, called the ringleader, urged the others to mutiny. Paul had encountered problems with this sailor before, so he wasn't surprised by the man's actions. The ringleader would not back down, but neither would Paul.

The ringleader and a few others were lowering a boat from the *Betsy* and planned to row to shore without permission. As the ringleader was about to

get in the boat, Paul confronted him. Drawing his sword, Paul thought he could frighten the men into obeying him. However, this just made the ringleader angry. He charged at Captain Paul with a club. Paul

John Paul Jones was a complex man with great military skill as well as a love for poetry.

During the 1700s, merchant ships were common sights in the harbors of the West Indies.

moved backward but came to an open hatchway. If he didn't stand his ground, he'd fall into the ship's hold and probably hurt himself.

Paul chose to stand up to the ringleader, especially since all eyes were on him. He didn't want to appear to be a coward in front of his crew. The ringleader rushed at Paul, who raised his arm and stabbed the ringleader with his sword, killing him.

Paul turned himself in to authorities in Tobago, but he was not arrested. Court was not in session at that time, but Paul knew that when court resumed, he would have to face a trial for the death of the ringleader. He feared that no one would believe his claim of self-defense. He also probably feared retaliation, or revenge, from the ringleader's family, who lived in Tobago.

Paul fled to the other side of the island, found an outbound ship, and boarded it. His plan was to stay out of sight until the initial outcry about the sailor's death faded. No one knows for sure where Paul went next—perhaps to his brother's home in Virginia—but within a few years, he would take on a new name and a new life in the Continental Navy. ◷

4 SAILING FOR THE UNITED STATES

⊸⚬⊱⚬⊶

By 1775, John Paul had traveled to Philadelphia, Pennsylvania, to seek a position in the new Continental Navy. He was now going by the name "John Paul Jones." No one is certain why he added "Jones" to his name or where it came from. He may have added it to avoid being connected to the murder trial in the West Indies. Along with his old name, Jones had left everything behind, including the money he had been saving for retirement. He had returned to Virginia in 1774, but now his older brother was dead. Jones had no family and no job in the American colonies, and he was relying on the charity of others to survive. It was time to start his life over again.

"America was my favorite country from the age

Because both the Declaration of Independence and the U.S. Constitution were created inside Independence Hall in Philadelphia, the site is often called the "birthplace of the nation."

37 ‿◞

American victory
British victory

CANADA

Quebec, 1775

Lake Superior

Montreal

Mass.

Fort Ticonderoga, 1777

Fort Ticonderoga, 1775

Lake Michigan

Lake Huron

Lake Ontario

Lake Erie

N.H.
Concord, 1775
Saratoga, 1777
Bunker Hill, 1775
Albany • Lexington, Boston
1775 Mass.
N.Y. Conn. Newport, 1778
R.I.
Pa.
Trenton, 1776 Battle of Long Island, 1776
Germantown, 1777 Princeton, 1777
Valley Forge • N.J.
Brandywine Creek, 1777

Ohio River

Appalachian Mountains

Md. Del.

Virginia
Richmond • Yorktown, 1781

BRITISH
NORTH AMERICA

Guilford Courthouse, 1781
N.C.
Cowpens, 1781 Kings Mountain, 1780
Camden, 1780
S.C.
Wilmington

Mississippi River

Atlantic
Ocean

Georgia
Charleston, 1780
Proclamation Line of 1763
Savannah, 1778

N
W   E
S

0   200 miles
0   200 kilometers

West Florida

East Florida

Major battles of the Revolution were fought throughout the colonies.

of 13, when I first saw it," Jones later wrote.

His arrival in Philadelphia proved to be perfect timing for a man who dreamed of fighting on the high seas. In 1775, Philadelphia, like many other

American cities, was buzzing with talk of war.

The American Revolutionary War had begun in the spring of 1775, and the Continental Congress was seeking ways to fight Great Britain on land and at sea. On October 13, Congress created the new Continental Navy and began searching for officers. It needed captains who could navigate well and lead sailors. Most of all, it needed leaders who were not afraid to take on the mighty British navy. It found one such captain in John Paul Jones.

At the start of the Revolutionary War, the British navy included nearly 300 ships. The colonies, meanwhile, were converting merchant ships and other small vessels into fighting ships. A naval committee established by the Continental Congress wanted to build 13 new warships for the young navy, but the money didn't exist in the country's budget—a problem that plagued the Americans throughout the war.

Another problem for the Continental Navy was privateers. Owned by private individuals rather than by Congress, privateers were small, armed ships crewed by sailors who captured enemy ships in exchange for the goods they could get. The goods included the captured ship itself, as well as any cargo it might be carrying.

Patrolling mostly in American waters, privateers were like pirates. They tended to go for the easy prizes—British merchant ships—rather than battle

Privateer recruiting offices lured young patriots with talk of easy money.

with big British warships. Not only did this ensure a bountiful haul, it also was safer for the crews because merchant ships were not as heavily armed as warships.

Serving on a privateer seemed more attractive to many sailors than serving in the Continental Navy. It seemed less dangerous, since the Continental Navy's number-one duty was fighting the mighty British warships. In addition, Continental Navy crews earned less of the take from captured ships than privateers did. So the Continental Navy had a difficult time recruiting. When faced with the idea of doing a more dangerous job for less pay, many sailors joined a privateer instead of the Continental Navy.

Privateers served a purpose, though. They disrupted British trade on the seas. Some of the supplies captured by privateers, such as weapons, clothing, and food, also helped the Continental Army.

Seeing their usefulness, several American colonies began working with privateers in the autumn of 1775. A few months later, Congress did the same. Hundreds of ships served as privateers during the Revolutionary War. Jones, however, detested the privateers. He was more interested in fighting the British navy than in lining his pockets with money.

Jones had become friends with a member of Congress named Joseph Hewes, a merchant from North Carolina. Hewes was part of the committee of Congress that was launching the new navy, and he arranged for Jones to be appointed as an officer in the new military branch.

Early in 1776, Jones joined a squadron of ships that raided British harbors in Nassau in the Bahamas and captured gunpowder and more than 70 cannons. Arms and ammunition were badly needed by the American military.

Later that year, Jones was given his own command on a ship called the *Providence*. The Marine Committee of the Continental Congress sent him his official orders:

> *We have ordered the Provisions & Stores you requested, to be sent on board the Sloop Providence which you Command under Authority of the United States of America, so that the said Sloop being now ready for Sea, you are to proceed immediately on a Cruize against our Enemies & we think in & about the Lattitude of Bermuda may proved the most favourable ground for your purpose. You are to be particularly attentive to protect, aid & assist all Vessells & property belonging to the States or Subjects thereof. It is equally your duty to Seize, take, Sink, Burn or destroy that of our Enemys. ... These things duely observed will recommend you to the attention & regard of this Committee.*

Among the Marine Committee's members were some of the most well-known leaders of the American Revolution, including John Hancock and

In C O N G R E S S.

The DELEGATES of the UNITED STATES of *New Hampshire, Massachusetts-Bay Rhode-Island, Connecticut, New York, New-Jersey, Pennsylvania, Delaware, Maryland, Virginia, North-Carolina, South-Carolina, and Georgia, TO*

John Paul Jones, Esquire,

WE, reposing especial Trust and Confidence in your Patriotism, Valour, Conduct, and Fidelity, DO, by these Presents, constitute and appoint you to be *Captain* — Navy — in the Service of the United States of North-America, fitted out for the Defence of American Liberty, and for repelling every hostile Invasion thereof. You are therefore carefully and diligently to discharge the Duty of *Captain* by doing and performing all manner of Things thereunto belonging. And we do strictly charge and require all Officers, Marines and Seamen under your Command, to be obedient to your Orders as *Captain* And you are to observe and follow such Orders and Directions from Time to Time as you shall receive from this or a future Congress of the United States, or Committee of Congress for that Purpose appointed, or Commander in Chief for the Time being of the Navy of the United States, or any other your superior Officer, according to the Rules and Discipline of War, the Usage of the Sea, and the Instructions herewith given you, in Pursuance of the Trust reposed in you. This Commission to continue in Force until revoked by this or a future Congress.

DATED at *Philadelphia October 10ᵗʰ 1776*

By Order of the CONGRESS,

John Hancock PRESIDENT

Robert Morris. In the orders, the committee made Jones's goal clear. Not only was he to do battle with British navy warships, he also was to capture British merchant ships traveling between Great Britain and North America.

Jones sailed on the *Providence* from Bermuda to Nova Scotia, capturing several trading ships. In October 1776, he captured a British transport ship carrying warm winter uniforms and other supplies

Jones's position in the Continental Navy became official in October 1776.

43

Dr. John K. Read, one of John Paul Jones's friends in the United States, introduced Jones to Dorothea Dandridge, who would become the love of Jones's life. Jones and Dandridge were never allowed to marry, though. When they met, Jones didn't have a job, and his savings were gone. With no way for Jones to show he could be a good provider, Dandridge's parents didn't believe the pair would be a good match. Dandridge ended up marrying Governor Patrick Henry of Virginia in 1777.

for the British army in North America. Jones sent these uniforms to General George Washington's army, which badly needed supplies and clothing. Jones's hard work wasn't going unnoticed, either. John Hancock suggested to fellow congressman Robert Morris that Jones be used as much as possible. He wrote:

I admire the spirited conduct of little Jones; pray push him out again. I know he does not love to be idle, & I am as certain you wish him to be constantly active, he is a fine fellow & he shall meet with every notice of mine & I am confident you will join me.

Jones had no intention of staying idle. He and other leaders in the Continental Navy were making bold plans to attack Great Britain in its own waters. In the Continental Congress, Robert Morris urged the navy's captains to plan attacks that would force the British navy to spend more time protecting its homeland than assaulting the shores of the American colonies. The young, poorly equipped Continental fleet simply could not defend itself against the much larger, established British fleet. The colonists' best hope for victory was to force the British fleet from an offensive position to a defensive one. Morris wrote:

> *It has long been clear to me that our Infant fleet cannot protect our own Coasts; and the only effectual relief it can afford us is to attack the enemies' defenceless places and thereby oblige them to station more of their Ships in their own Countries, or to keep them employed in following ours, and either way we are relieved.*

Robert Morris was one of the 56 men to sign the Declaration of Independence in 1776.

Jones agreed to take the challenge. He planned to raid British seaports and destroy British ships in their harbors. ❧

Chapter

5 FIGHTING IN GREAT BRITAIN

❧∽✕∽❧

In 1777, Jones was given command of the ship *Ranger* and a crew of about 150 sailors from Portsmouth, New Hampshire. So far, most of the fighting in the Revolutionary War had been on American soil or in the colonies' waterways or near their coastlines. For the first time, Jones was taking the fight to the British.

He sailed first to France, which had joined the United States as an ally in its fight against Britain. Jones would launch his attacks on Britain from the south, from French ports.

Jones's voyage to the British Isles began badly. He had to deal with disloyal crew members and even threatened one sailor with a pistol to stop a mutiny. In Ireland's Belfast Bay, Jones tried to attack the British

One of the first ships commissioned, or ordered, by the young Continental Navy, the Ranger *was built in 1777 and launched from Badger's Island in Kittery, Maine.*

John Paul Jones's *appointment to the* Ranger *was published in the* Journal of Congress *next to some other very important news. Congress had approved the United States of America's new flag. "Resolved, That the Flag of the thirteen United States be thirteen stripes, alternate red and white; that the union be thirteen stars, white in a blue field, representing a new constellation." Jones was known to fly a British flag on his ship to trick the enemy, but once he engaged in battle, he raised this newly adopted flag.*

warship *Drake*, but bad weather forced him back out to sea.

"The weather now became so very stormy and severe and the sea ran so high that I was obliged to take shelter under the south shore of Scotland," Jones said later in a letter.

Jones made a bold decision. Instead of going on with the mission as planned, he would sail for the port of Whitehaven, England, not far from his boyhood home. Hundreds of British ships were at rest there, and Jones made plans to raid the harbor and set fire to the wooden ships. But residents of Whitehaven found out about Jones's plan and drove off his raiding party before it could do much damage. Jones was able to light a coal ship on fire, though. This sight in the harbor alone was enough to inspire fear in the townspeople. Jones later remembered:

The inhabitants began to appear in thousands and individuals ran hastily towards us. I stood between them and the

Betsy Ross Flag 1777

Ship of Fire with a pistol in my hand and ordered them to retire which they did without precipitation. The flames had already caught the rigging and began to ascend the main mast. The sun was a full hour's march above the horizon, and as sleep no longer ruled the world, it was time to retire.

Betsy Ross sewed the first official American flag in 1777.

Desperate for action, Jones raided the estate of the Earl of Selkirk near Whitehaven. He planned to kidnap the earl and trade him to the British in exchange for captured American prisoners.

As they approached the earl's estate, Jones and his men happened upon the earl's gardener. Jones pretended he and his men were British officials looking for able-bodied men to serve in the Royal Navy. The man reacted just as Jones thought he would, running off to warn the men on the estate that they were about to be taken into the service of the Royal Navy. Promptly, they all disappeared, leaving the earl unprotected.

The plan would have worked perfectly if the earl had been home. Jones soon learned he had gone on an extended trip. Determined not to leave empty-handed, Jones's men robbed the earl's mansion, stealing valuable silver and even taking the family's teapot—the very symbol of British life. But Jones didn't participate in the theft. He had not come to England to steal teapots. He made up his mind to find the *Drake* again and attack her.

John Paul Jones was not a thief, and the fact that his crew had stolen silver from the earl of Selkirk bothered him for many years. Finally, in 1784, Jones returned the silver to its rightful owner.

Jones's *Ranger* met the *Drake* in Ireland's Belfast Bay on April 24, 1778. Jones tried a trick he

Contrary to this artist's rendering, Jones did not meet Lady Selkirk when his men looted her estate.

had played many times before. He pretended the *Ranger* was a British merchant ship. He even had his crew fly the British flag, and Jones wore the uniform of a British naval officer.

The captain of the *Drake* sent out a small vessel to meet with the *Ranger* and its crew. The British officer and the others on the small boat accepted Jones's invitation to board what they thought was a

Both the Drake
and the Ranger
*suffered losses
during their
historic battle.*

British merchant ship. They were easily captured and taken below deck.

Realizing something was terribly wrong, the remaining crew of the *Drake* headed out of the harbor. For much of the afternoon, the *Drake* and the *Ranger* sailed around one another, trying to get in the best fighting position possible. As the two ships came closer, the sailors on both ships prepared for battle. Crowds on the shore watched as the two ships circled each other and exchanged cannon fire.

Jones had trained his gunners well. They worked in teams of six or more, aiming, loading, and firing the huge guns. They blasted away at the sails and masts of the *Drake* until the British ship could no longer sail.

Jones also ordered crew members to climb high into the rigging of the *Ranger* and fire their guns down on the decks of the *Drake*. Any British sailor who didn't take cover risked being shot. Jones directed the fighting from the deck of the *Ranger*. Around him, his sailors were falling dead or wounded. However, the destruction on the British ship *Drake* was worse, and both the British captain and his second in command were mortally wounded. After about an hour of heavy fighting, one of the British officers called out, "Quarter," the word for surrender, and pulled down the ship's flag from the staff.

Ezra Green, the surgeon aboard the Ranger, treated wounded sailors from both the Ranger and the Drake. Performing surgery onboard a warship was difficult and dirty. Sponges were "cleaned" and readied for the next patient by dipping them in a pail of bloody water. Anesthetic was in short supply, too, and often surgery was done without any pain medication. In some cases, sailors bit on a bullet during surgery to help ease the pain. The expression "bite the bullet" is used today when telling someone to be tough and bear the pain.

The moment was a historic one. For the first time ever, an American navy ship had defeated a British warship in a one-on-one battle—and, more amazingly, in British waters. Jones took possession of the *Drake* with 133 prisoners and sailed back to France, flying the U.S. flag.

6 SAILING ON THE BONHOMME RICHARD

❧❧❧

The capture of the *Drake* alarmed the British public, who had come to think of its navy as unbeatable. British newspapers were filled with stories about "the pirate Jones." The British navy sent ships out looking for him. In British seaports, local militias tried to build up their defenses, expecting Jones to attack at any time.

"What was done, however, is sufficient to show that not all their boasted navy can protect their own coasts and that the scenes of distress which they have occasioned in America may soon be brought home to their own doors," Jones wrote after the capture of the *Drake*.

Yet despite Jones's victory, the war at sea was going badly for the United States. In 1778 alone, the

Jones's most famous ship, the Bonhomme Richard *(French for "Poor Richard"), was named after a publication by American statesman, philosopher, and inventor Benjamin Franklin, shown here.*

Continental Navy lost 15 ships to the British. The United States was so desperate for new ships that it tried turning merchant vessels into warships by adding more weapons and cutting holes in the sides of the ships for cannons to fire through.

When Jones reached France, a letter from Benjamin Franklin awaited him. Franklin was an American representative charged with securing financial aid and other support from France for the American Revolution. In the letter, Franklin told Jones that his great victory against the *Drake* had earned him command of the *Indien*, a new ship being built for the Continental Navy. Jones's victorious *Ranger*, its mission now completed, sailed back to New Hampshire with its crew.

"I have the pleasure of informing you that it is proposed to give you command of the great ship we have built at Amsterdam," Franklin wrote.

Antoine de Sartine, a French minister, was making the arrangements to give Jones the ship, Franklin said. Jones had been promised such commands before and been disappointed. This time was no different. When Jones arrived to speak with Sartine, all promises made regarding his command of the *Indien* evaporated. Not only was the ship not finished, the Netherlands would not allow it to sail under an American flag.

The Netherlands remained neutral in the

American Revolution and the wars between France and Great Britain. Because their country was neutral, sailors from the Netherlands were allowed to sail and trade with France and Great Britain without fear of being attacked by either of these nations' powerful navies. The Netherlands didn't want to anger Britain by helping America. This would mean risking the safety of its ships on the open seas.

Jones was angry, but there was nothing he could do but search for another ship and get back

The Bonhomme Richard *was built in France in 1765 for the purpose of trading goods between France and ports in the Far East.*

out to sea. In 1779, Jones took command of an old French ship called the *Duc de Duras* and had it rebuilt to carry more cannons. The French minister bought the ship for Jones to try to make amends for failing to deliver the *Indien.*

Jones gave the *Duc de Duras* a new name in honor of his friend Benjamin Franklin. Franklin's *Poor Richard's Almanack*, an annual publication containing information on such topics as weather and astronomy, was popular in France, where it was called *Les Maxims du Bonhomme Richard.* So Jones called his ship *Bonhomme Richard*, or "Poor Richard."

Jones planned to lead a squadron of five ships (the *Bonhomme Richard*, the *Alliance*, the *Pallas*, the *Vengeance*, and the *Cerf*) in an attack on the west coast of England. At the same time, a French fleet and 40,000 troops would invade England from the east. Plans for invasion fell apart, however, because of an outbreak of smallpox and typhus aboard the French ships.

Still, Jones went ahead with his voyage to Great

John Paul Jones used many clever ideas to disguise his ships and give him the element of surprise when attacking the British. In the case of the Bonhomme Richard, Jones had the ship painted black to disguise the vessel's gun ports. This practice was considered "ungentlemanly" by the British code of warfare and helped earn Jones his reputation in Britain as a pirate and traitor to his British homeland.

Britain from France on August 14, 1779. His crew of 380 included sailors from France, Bengal, Ireland, Norway, Switzerland, Italy, Scotland, England, and India, as well as America. His goal was to attack a fleet of 41 British merchant ships that would be sailing off the coast of England. Such ships made valuable prizes, if captured, because their cargo and the ships them- selves were worth a great deal of money. However, merchant fleets were almost always escorted by British warships.

Jones's confidence in his own abilities as an officer was seen as arrogance by some crew members, which caused tension aboard Jones's ship.

As was often the case, Jones encountered several problems on the voyage. Every trip seemed to include crew members who refused to obey orders. Deserters were another problem. Once they spied their home- land, some of the Irish and English crew members simply left, never to return to the ship. Unfortunately, these deserters didn't keep quiet. They warned their countrymen that John Paul Jones and his fleet were on their way.

Jones planned to sail the *Bonhomme Richard*

past Ireland's west coast and around Scotland to the north before coming down England's east coast, inflicting terror along the way. One of the places he planned to attack was Scotland's capital city of Edinburgh. As he approached Edinburgh's port at Leith, Jones wrote a note to be delivered to Leith's leader.

"My intention," Jones wrote, "is only to demand your contribution towards the reimbursement which Britain owes to the much injured citizens of America."

He also wrote that Great Britain had treated the United States cruelly, and now Leith would know how that felt. Jones said he didn't wish to hurt any Scottish citizens, but he would burn the town to the ground if his demands weren't met.

"Before I proceed to that stern duty as an officer, my duty as a man induces me to propose to you by the means of a reasonable ransom to prevent such scenes of horror and distress," Jones wrote.

Jones intended to hold six of the city's council-

> *Some of the crew onboard the Bonhomme Richard had been American prisoners in British jails. John Paul Jones always worried about American prisoners and helped whenever he could to free them. The freed Americans on the Bonhomme Richard had been released in exchange for British prisoners held by Jones. Once released, many of the former American prisoners were happy to fight alongside Jones and gain revenge against the British for their cruel treatment.*

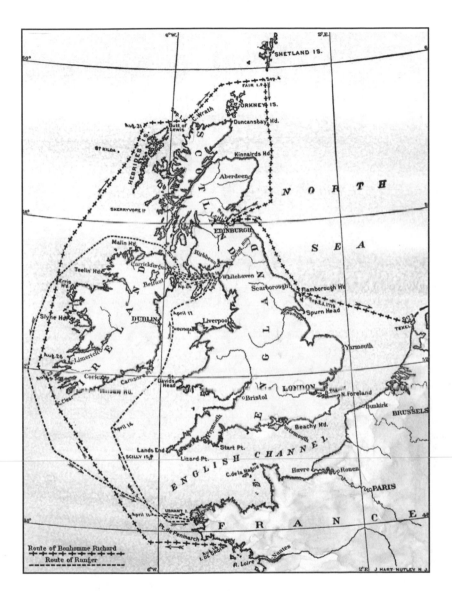

men as hostages. Half of the ransom he mentioned would be paid in cash and the other half promised in a written note. When the cash was received, Jones would release three hostages. The other three would

John Paul Jones sailed the Ranger *and the* Bonhomme Richard *in British waters.*

Jones is portrayed as a fearsome pirate in this British cartoon.

be held until the remaining debt was paid in full. Bad weather forced Jones to abandon his plan, though. As the wind and rain suddenly beat down on his fleet, Jones headed back out to calmer seas.

Despite spending six weeks sailing around the coast of Great Britain, Jones captured only a few ships. He was disappointed, but what he didn't realize was that his very presence was making a huge impression on the people of Great Britain.

Britons were angry when they realized their shores weren't as safe as they had once believed they were. News of John Paul Jones appeared all over the British newspapers. Maybe, people said, this war with America hadn't been such a good idea after all.

While people in Great Britain continued to talk and worry about Jones, the biggest battle of his career was still to come. 🐚

7 BATTLE WITH THE *SERAPIS*

❧⌘❧

On the afternoon of September 23, 1779, Jones and the crew of the *Bonhomme Richard* spotted the British merchant fleet and two navy ships—the *Serapis* and the *Countess of Scarborough*—near Filey Bay, on the east coast of England. Jones knew this was his chance to attack.

In the 18th century, ships communicated with each other by a system of flashing lights. Jones signaled to the other ships in his squadron to stay close and prepare to attack. Instead, two of his ships simply ignored his orders and sailed off. The other took after the *Countess of Scarborough*.

The *Bonhomme Richard* sailed on alone to challenge the British ship *Serapis*. As Jones got closer to the ship, he could see British Captain Richard

John Paul Jones led the fight against the much larger British warship Serapis.

Pearson nailing his ship's flag to the staff. Captains signaled surrender by lowering their ship's flag, so Pearson was letting his crew know that he did not plan on surrendering.

As the sun began to set, the two vessels were close enough for the sailors on each ship to call out to each other. Pearson shouted out a demand for the other ship to identify itself. At first, Jones said his ship was the *Princess Royal*, the name of a British ship. Pearson knew this was a lie, and when he demanded another answer, Jones said nothing. Then cannons on both ships began firing.

The two ships sailed only about 25 yards (23 meters) apart, making the men on deck easy targets. Many were killed in the opening shots of the battle, yet the fighting continued.

"The battle being thus begun was Continued with Unremitting fury," Jones later wrote in his account of the event.

At first, the battle went badly for Jones and the sailors on the *Bonhomme Richard*. British cannonballs tore holes in the side of Jones's ship, and fires broke out on the deck. The *Serapis* was a faster ship

> *Bitter because he wasn't in charge, Pierre Landais, the French captain of the Alliance, almost constantly ignored John Paul Jones's orders. At one point during the battle with the Serapis, Landais even had the Alliance fire upon the Bonhomme Richard. Because of this, Jones and Landais remained hated enemies for the rest of their lives.*

and easier to maneuver. As the two ships vied for the best fighting position, Pearson used his ship's advantage to keep Jones on the defensive. Jones could see he was losing.

Night had fallen, and the battle continued, lit by the moon and flashes of the ships' guns. Jones knew he could no longer exchange cannon fire with the British ship. The *Bonhomme Richard's* guns were badly damaged. Jones's only chance was to get close enough to the *Serapis* so his sailors could jump over the railing and fight in hand-to-hand combat.

As Jones steered the *Bonhomme Richard* in close to the enemy, his officers threw thick, heavy

The Bonhomme Richard *and the* Serapis *battled into the night.*

ropes and grappling hooks at the *Serapis* and began pulling the two ships together, locking them side by side. Armed with a variety of weapons, including pistols and swords, the *Bonhomme Richard's* crew readied to jump aboard the *Serapis*.

Still, the British gunners continued firing, sending cannonballs all the way through the *Bonhomme Richard* and out the other side. Others on the *Serapis* started swinging axes to cut away the ropes thrown onto their ship by the *Bonhomme Richard's* crew. When he saw this, Jones abandoned the plan to board the *Serapis*.

The situation went from bad to worse for Jones's crew. By now, both ships were on fire, and the *Bonhomme Richard's* hold was filling with water. In the confusion of the battle, some of Jones's officers thought he had been killed. The ship's carpenter, John Gunnison, found the person he believed was the highest ranking officer still alive—Henry Gardner—and alerted him that the ship was going to sink. Gardner decided to surrender, yelling, "Quarter!" He also ordered the *Bonhomme Richard's* flag to be taken down from the staff. When Jones saw what was happening, he became enraged.

"Who are those rascals?" he shouted. "Shoot them! Kill them!"

Jones aimed his pistol at Gunnison, but the gun wouldn't

The British merchant ships escorted by the Countess of Scarborough and the Serapis carried rope, canvas, timber, and other supplies needed by the British navy for its warships. These supplies were also needed by the Continental Navy, which made the merchant ships attractive targets for Jones and his squadron.

fire. Frustrated and angry, Jones threw the pistol across the ship at Gardner's head, knocking the man unconscious.

With the two ships side by side, Pearson could see the confusion on the deck of Jones's ship. Shouting across the railing, he asked Jones if he was surrendering. It was then that Jones supposedly told the British captain the battle was far from over by stating his now famous line: "I have not yet begun to fight!"

Jones had one advantage. He had wisely stationed a group of men high in his ship's rigging and ordered them to fire their guns down on the deck of the *Serapis*. A sailor named William Hamilton tossed a grenade across to the *Serapis*, where it bounced and exploded near a supply of gunpowder. The explosion set off huge fires and nearly cut down the mast of the *Serapis*.

Now, it was Pearson who was in trouble. His ship was on fire, and his mast was about to topple. He had lost about half of his sailors. This time it was Pearson

During the battle with the Serapis, about 100 English sailors were being held prisoner below the deck of the Bonhomme Richard. As water filled the hold, the prisoners were in danger of drowning. John Burbank, one of the Bonhomme Richard's officers, felt sorry for the prisoners and set them free to go above deck. The prisoners could have caused trouble for their captors, but they were so grateful that they actually helped pump water out of the sinking ship.

Hand-to-hand combat turned the battle against the Serapis in Jones's favor.

who decided it was time to surrender.

"I ask for quarter, sir," Pearson called out.

Jones could hardly believe what he was hearing.

He demanded that Pearson take down his flag

Jones graciously accepted Pearson's surrender after hours of intense fighting.

immediately, and then he ordered his men to stop fighting. To make the surrender official, Pearson presented Jones with his sword.

"You have fought like a hero, sir," Jones said.

Both the *Serapis* and the *Bonhomme Richard* lost about half their crews in the bloody battle, and despite the victory, the *Bonhomme Richard* was too badly damaged to save.

Jones ordered what was left of his crew to board the *Serapis*. Together they watched their old ship slowly sink beneath the waves.

Jones was the first American to capture a British warship of any size. He had proven that the British navy was not invincible. With the *Bonhomme Richard* gone, Jones sailed the *Serapis* quickly away, reaching a friendly port in the Netherlands on October 3, 1779. ❧

Chapter

8 A Hero on Two Continents

In Great Britain, Jones's victory created a panic. The British people feared that an invasion by U.S. and French ships was sure to follow.

Jones wrote a letter to Ben Franklin detailing the battle with the *Serapis*. The news reached Congress and was published in newspapers across the United States. John Paul Jones was a hero to the people of the young country.

He also was well known on the streets of Amsterdam, having docked there with the captured *Serapis* after his victory, but he wouldn't be welcome there for long. The Netherlands still feared British reaction to anything that might be considered help for the Americans. Now, here was this man the British considered an American pirate parading through the

People throughout the United States and Europe praised John Paul Jones's heroism in poems, songs, and paintings such as this.

In 1779, King Louis XVI of France named John Paul Jones a chevalier (similar to being knighted).

streets of Amsterdam. Jones's presence put the Netherlands in an uncomfortable spot.

British naval crews knew where Jones was hiding. Respecting the Netherlands' neutral position, British ships waited just outside the country's waters to capture Jones when he left for France. Jones knew the British were waiting for him. He waited until after Christmas when the wind changed direction and blew the British ships away from their current locations. Jones then sailed his new ship, the *Alliance*, right past them.

In France, Jones discovered that his victory against the *Serapis* had made him a hero on the European continent, too. France and Great Britain had been enemies for years, and the French enjoyed seeing the British navy take a beating. Everywhere Jones went in France, he was greeted by cheering crowds. He was applauded at parties and at the opera. King Louis XVI of France presented him with a sword in honor of his victory. In America, the Continental Congress passed a resolution honoring him, and General George Washington wrote Jones a letter praising him for his "brilliant action."

Although Jones was enjoying life in France, his crew was angry. They had not been paid for their work before and during the battle with the *Serapis*. Jones had not been paid either, but as a hero, he was invited to parties and dinners and didn't need the money. Meanwhile, his crew was not invited to these events, didn't have warm clothes, and sat on a boat that was being overrun by rats.

Initially, Jones did try to get his crew its money, but he was easily distracted by all the attention he was getting. He loved being a hero. He enjoyed the parties, the opera, the ballet, and all the other events he was invited to now that he was a celebrity.

By June 1, 1780, Ben Franklin had grown tired of hearing about Jones's behavior. The crew members of the *Alliance* had contacted Franklin and asked him to relieve Jones of his command. They asked to sail back to America with another captain at the helm.

Franklin told the crew they should be delighted to sail with a man as brave as Jones; he told Jones to quit flirting with the

Because the American government had very little money following the Revolutionary War and had a great many debts, Congress would not vote to pay the crew of the Bonhomme Richard until 1848, nearly 70 years after their famous voyage. By then, all the crew members were dead, and the money went to their descendants.

The Alliance *was launched in 1778 and remained in service for more than 130 years.*

French ladies and get his ship loaded with supplies desperately needed by the Continental Army. Franklin also warned Jones that his crew was very angry with him.

"I see you are likely to have a great deal of trouble," Franklin said. "It requires prudence. I wish you well through it. You have shown your abilities in fighting. You now have the opportunity of showing the other necessary part of the character of a great chief, your abilities in governing."

Jones set to work getting his ship and crew ready to sail back to the United States. While Jones was on shore on June 12, Pierre Landais, the former captain of the *Alliance*, took over the ship and set sail for America. The crew got what it wanted: Landais instead of Jones.

Though the French were prepared to get the ship back, Jones decided to let it go, which angered Franklin. Not only had Jones just let the *Alliance* go, the ship had left most of the supplies—weapons, ammunition, and clothing—the Continental Army needed. Jones also shifted the blame to French officials for letting the ship go, rather than taking the blame himself. Franklin scolded Jones:

> *If you had stayed aboard where your duty lay, instead of coming to Paris, you would not have lost your ship. Now you blame them as having deserted you in recovering her ... Hereafter, if you should observe on occasion to give your officers and friends a little more praise than is their due, and confess more fault than you can justly be charged with, you will only become the sooner for it, a great captain. Criticizing and censuring almost*

Jones enjoyed his newfound celebrity status among Parisian high society.

everyone you have to do with, will diminish friends, increase enemies, and thereby hurt your affairs.

Franklin quickly worked with the French to get another ship for Jones. The supplies still needed to reach the Continental Army.

"Now you have *Ariel;* for heaven's sake, load her as heavily as she can bear, and sail! I will see to moving the rest," Franklin wrote to Jones.

Yet Jones still dragged his feet. He said he wanted to make sure he and his crew got the money they were owed for their work on the *Bonhomme Richard*. He also wanted to make sure there were plans for him to come back across the Atlantic Ocean and continue to intimidate the British.

But Jones's great victory against the *Serapis* was his last battle of the war. He would see action again, but not while serving in the Continental Navy. ✍

9 ADVENTURES AFTER THE WAR

Chapter

‿❧❧❧‿

Jones finally returned to the United States in February 1781. The weapons, ammunition, and clothing he brought turned out to be useful to the Continental Army. General Washington's troops marched south to Virginia that summer for what proved to be the last major campaign of the Revolutionary War. On October 19, 1781, a large British army surrendered at Yorktown, Virginia. The United States had won its independence.

After the war, Jones hoped to help lead the navy of the United States. Even before the end of the war, he had told Congressman Robert Morris he wanted to have a part in building a strong naval force, one that could rival the navies of Great Britain and France in strength.

The British signaled their surrender after the seige of Yorktown in 1781, ending the Revolutionary War.

"Our navy has not only been put in bad hands, it has been unwisely deployed," Jones wrote. "It has served to enrich a few ignorant individuals and has done almost nothing for our cause. If my feeble voice is heard when I return to Philadelphia our navy matters will assume a better face."

Jones wanted to build an American navy in which officers were appointed based on their skills rather than on their connections with influential people. He also wanted to hire good shipbuilders— again not giving someone a job simply because a congressman was his friend or owed him a favor.

Jones believed the United States needed a permanent force of naval officers and a naval academy to train them. He wrote to members of Congress, "In a time of Peace, it is necessary to prepare, and be always prepared for War by Sea." However, Congress faced many other pressing problems and had little interest in supporting a navy during peacetime. It also didn't have the money it needed to build the kind of navy Jones wanted. In fact, Congress was trying to sell the ships it did have in order to raise money to keep the new nation going.

Jones spent a full year in

After the Revolutionary War, the United States didn't have much of a navy left. During the war, the Continental Navy included 57 ships. Thirty-four of them were captured, sunk, or destroyed. Four more were lost at sea.

oh that barn!

In 1787, Congress had a copper medal made to celebrate Jones's victory against the Serapis.

Portsmouth, New Hampshire, waiting for the completion of the *America*, the largest warship built in the United States at that time, hoping to be named its captain. But in the end, the ship was given to France. Unfortunately, Jones was still considered an outsider by some members of Congress and various

Thomas Jefferson was the third president of the United States, serving from 1801 to 1809.

officials in the American navy. He was a Scotsman, not an American citizen. He wasn't rich, and he held no land. He also wasn't among the elite American captains. As a result, even though his victory against the *Serapis* had earned him heroic status on two continents, Jones would never be given control of another American ship.

Jones remained hopeful his country would eventually establish a strong navy, but he found nothing but disappointment. In November 1787, he traveled to Paris, where he met with Thomas Jefferson, who was serving as the American minister to France. Jefferson knew that Empress Catherine II (Catherine the Great) of Russia was hiring experienced naval commanders for the Russian navy. Although Catherine was known as a cruel leader, Jefferson believed Jones could gain valuable experience serving in the Russian navy. Jones could then use that experience to strengthen the American navy once Congress was ready to fund it. "I consider this officer as the principal hope of our future efforts on the ocean," Jefferson wrote to a friend in describing Jones.

Jones wasn't sure if he wanted to join the Russian navy. The United States had just adopted its new Constitution. Congress soon would realize it needed to establish a navy, Jones believed. But the call of the sea and possible glory remained a temptation to Jones, too. He decided to take a chance and accept the position Jefferson offered. Jones was appointed a rear admiral in the Russian navy.

The Constitutional Convention met in Philadelphia the summer of 1787. Delegates to the convention signed the new U.S. Constitution September 17, 1787, but the document still needed to be ratified by 9 of the country's 13 states before it would become the law of the land. The ninth state to ratify the Constitution was New Hampshire on June 21, 1788.

Catherine the Great ruled Russia from 1762 to 1796.

Russia was at war with Turkey, and Jones joined the battle. He took command of a fleet of Russian ships in the Black Sea and defeated the

Turks in a series of battles in 1788.

However, Jones was a stranger in the Russian navy. He could not speak Russian. And since he hadn't trained with the seamen he commanded, he had made few friends. Now 40 years old, he wasn't as healthy as he had been in the past. Years of sleeping just three hours a night and living on the seas had worn him down. Yet, when he developed a lung infection, Jones didn't let it slow him down.

As Jones won battles for Russia, other officers grew jealous of his success and made sure he did not receive credit for his victories. They watched Jones closely, hoping he would make a mistake, and Jones knew it. He told his contact with the Russian naval leadership:

> *My situation here is very delicate and critical. I have people around me who appear to be on their guard, and if I make the slightest mistake, even when following their advice, I was given to understand today that they would consider themselves only as passengers.*

Soon, Empress Catherine decided that her navy no longer needed the American naval hero and dismissed him. Jones left the Russian navy in 1789. He had fought his last battle. ✍

Dillen Rogers

Chapter

10 THE FINAL YEARS

⌒⌒⌒

Jones returned to Paris discouraged by his experience in Russia. He even tried to get Empress Catherine to change her mind and let him sail for her again, but she wanted nothing to do with him.

Things weren't much better for Jones in Paris. Just a few years earlier, he had been treated as a hero there, but now he was a sad and nearly forgotten man. Old friends no longer had time for him. They didn't invite him to lavish parties anymore, and when he tried to drop in anyway, he was not welcomed. Eventually, Jones settled in to a quiet, lonely life.

By 1792, Jones's health was beginning to fail. He often suffered from pneumonia, likely a result of his hard life at sea. He was tired, and he no

French sculptor Jean Antoine Houdon created this marble bust of John Paul Jones in 1780.

John Paul Jones spent his final days in this apartment building in Paris.

longer cared to eat. He developed jaundice, a yellowing of the skin caused by the liver's inability to process bodily wastes effectively.

In July 1792, Jones sent a message to the American ambassador to France, Gouverneur Morris.

He told Morris that he was near death and needed assistance to make sure his affairs were in order.

Morris came to Jones's apartment on July 18, 1792, and helped him prepare his will. Jones left all his possessions to his two surviving sisters. That evening, Jones died alone in his bedroom. He was 45 years old.

Shortly after Jones died, a package arrived at his apartment from Thomas Jefferson. Jones had kept in contact with Jefferson, who now was the U.S. secretary of state. Jones always had been concerned about the plight of American prisoners. Late in life, his focus had shifted to American prisoners being held in Algiers, North Africa. Jones had told Jefferson he wanted to lead a fleet to stop pirates along the North African coast from imprisoning sailors from American merchant ships.

When 13 American sailors who had gone through this ordeal wrote to Congress asking for help, Congress finally listened. It decided to send a delegation, or group of representatives, to Algiers to negotiate the sailors' freedom. Immediately, Jefferson thought of Jones. He would be the perfect person to lead the delegation. Unfortunately, Jefferson's message asking for help in the matter arrived after Jones's death.

After a simple funeral attended by a few friends and dignitaries, John Paul Jones was buried in a

The names of the Jones's ships are carved into the floor around his tomb at the U.S. Naval Academy.

cemetery outside Paris. There he rested for more than 100 years, as the United States grew to become a great naval power.

The U.S. Navy traced its traditions back to

Jones's daring exploits during the Revolutionary War. In 1905, his body was moved to a place of honor at the U.S. Naval Academy in Annapolis, Maryland. It was a fitting tribute to Jones's achievements. During the desperate times of the Revolutionary War, he showed great courage, leadership, and a determination to fight. His fearless raids on Great Britain helped win American independence. In the early 1900s, President Theodore Roosevelt declared, "Every officer in our navy should know by heart the deeds of John Paul Jones."

In 1905, General Horace Porter located John Paul Jones's original gravesite. The site proved difficult to find, as the Paris cemetery in which Jones was buried had subsequently been used as a vegetable garden, a dumping ground for dead animals, and a building lot. An autopsy indicated that the body was likely Jones's, based on height, weight, age, and other factors, but no definitive proof of the body's identity exists.

The inscription on John Paul Jones's tomb at the U.S. Naval Academy says it best: "He gave our Navy its earliest traditions of heroism and victory."

JONES'S LIFE

1761

Begins career at sea as an apprentice aboard the *Friendship;* visits his older brother, William, in Fredericksburg, Virginia

1747

Born John Paul on July 6 in Kirkbean, Kirkcudbright, Scotland

1764

Takes a job aboard the slave ship *King George*

1755

1756–63

The Seven Years' War is fought; Britain defeats France

1764

James Hargreaves creates the spinning jenny, a mechanical spinning wheel

WORLD EVENTS

1767

Resigns from
Two Friends

1766

Joins the slave
ship *Two Friends*
as first mate

1768

Navigates the *John*
back to Scotland
following the sudden
deaths of its captain
and first mate

1768

British explorer
Captain James Cook
leaves England for a
three-year exploration
of the Pacific

JONES'S LIFE

1772

Takes command
of the merchant
ship *Betsy*

1770

Stops a mutiny
of the *John;*
flogs the ship's
carpenter for
his role in the
uprising

1773

Attempting to stop
another mutiny,
kills a sailor in self-
defense; flees to
avoid arrest and
trial

1770

1769

British explorer
Captain James
Cook reaches
New Zealand

1772

Poland is parti-
tioned for the first
time, between
Russia, Prussia, and
Austria

WORLD EVENTS

1775

Joins Continental
Navy as first lieu-
tenant aboard the
Alfred; now goes by
the name "John
Paul Jones"

1774

Returns to
Fredericksburg,
Virginia, to visit
his brother

1776

Takes command
of the sloop
Providence

1774

King Louis XV of
France dies, and his
grandson, Louis XVI,
is crowned

1775

The first British
yacht club, the
Royal Thames
Yacht Club, is
founded

1776

Scottish econo-
mist Adam Smith
publishes *The
Wealth of Nations,*
heralding the
beginning of mod-
ern economics

JONES'S LIFE

1779

As captain of
Bonhomme Richard,
defeats *Serapis* off
the coast of England

1778

As captain of *Ranger*,
defeats British ship
Drake near Ireland

1781

Returns to the United
States with supplies for
the Continental Army

1780

1779

Jan Ingenhousz of the
Netherlands discovers
that plants release
oxygen when exposed
to sunlight

1783

Joseph Michel and
Jacques Étienne
Montgolfier become
the first human
beings to fly with
their invention of
the hot-air balloon

WORLD EVENTS

1789

Resigns from the Russian navy and moves to Paris

1792

Dies in Paris on July 18

1788

Becomes rear admiral in the Russian navy; wins battle against Turkish navy in the Black Sea

1790

1788

The *Times* newspaper in London is founded

1791

Austrian composer Wolfgang Amadeus Mozart dies

1786

The British government announces its plans to make Australia a penal colony

DATE OF BIRTH: July 6, 1747

BIRTHPLACE: Kirkbean, Kirkcudbright, Scotland

FATHER: John Paul Sr.

MOTHER: Jean MacDuff Paul

EDUCATION: Scottish public schools until age 12

SPOUSE: none

DATE OF MARRIAGE: none

CHILDREN: none

DATE OF DEATH: July 18, 1792

PLACE OF BURIAL: Buried in Paris; his body was later moved to the U.S. Naval Academy, Annapolis, Maryland

Additional Resources

In the Library

Alphin, Elaine Marie. *I Have Not Yet Begun to Fight: A Story About John Paul Jones.* Minneapolis: Lerner Publishing Group, 2004.

Hossell, Karen Price. *John Paul Jones.* St. Louis, Mo.: Heinemann Library, 2004.

Ingram, Scott. *John Paul Jones.* San Diego: Blackbirch Press, 2002.

Lutz, Norma Jean. *John Paul Jones: Father of the U.S. Navy.* Philadelphia: Chelsea House, 2000.

Tibbits, Alison Davis. *John Paul Jones: Father of the American Navy.* Berkeley Heights, N.J.: Enslow Publishers, 2002.

Look for more Signature Lives
BOOKS ABOUT THIS ERA:

Abigail Adams: *Courageous Patriot and First Lady*
ISBN 0-7565-0981-5

Alexander Hamilton: *Founding Father and Statesman*
ISBN 0-7565-0827-4

Benedict Arnold: *From Patriot to Traitor*
ISBN 0-7565-0825-8

Benjamin Franklin: *Scientist and Statesman*
ISBN 0-7565-0826-6

Ethan Allen: *Green Mountain Rebel*
ISBN 0-7565-0824-X

John Hancock: *Signer for Independence*
ISBN 0-7565-0828-2

Mercy Otis Warren: *Author and Historian*
ISBN 0-7565-0982-3

Phillis Wheatley: *Slave and Poet*
ISBN 0-7565-0984-X

Samuel Adams: *Patriot and Statesman*
ISBN 0-7565-0823-1

Thomas Paine: *Great Writer of the Revolution*
ISBN 0-7565-0830-4

Martha Washington: *First Lady of the United States*
ISBN 0-7565-0983-1

On the Web

For more information on *John Paul Jones*, use FactHound to track down Web sites related to this book.

1. Go to *www.facthound.com*
2. Type in a search word related to this book or this book ID: 0756508290
3. Click on the *Fetch It* button.

FactHound will find the best Web sites for you.

Historic Sites

John Paul Jones House
43 Middle Street
Portsmouth, NH 03801
603/436-8420
To view the house and gardens where Jones stayed in 1777 and 1782.

U.S. Naval Academy Chapel
101 Cooper Road
Annapolis, MD 21402-5027
410/293-1100
To view the tomb of John Paul Jones.

ally
a group, such as a country, favorably linked to another by a treaty or agreement

apprentice
a person who works for and learns from a skilled tradesperson for a certain amount of time

first mate
a ship officer ranking below the captain

grappling hooks
curved pieces of iron usually attached to ropes and used to anchor ships

magazine
a room aboard a ship where ammunition and explosives are stored

mast
a long pole that supports the sails and rigging on a ship

mutiny
when a group refuses to follow the orders of its leader

navigate
to direct the course of a ship through water

neutral
not taking sides in a disagreement

patriots
American colonists who wanted their independence from Britain

rigging
the system of ropes used aboard a ship to set and work the sails

sloop
a small warship with just one mast

Source Notes

Chapter 1
Page 11, line 18: Evan Thomas. *John Paul Jones: Sailor, Hero, Father of the American Navy*. New York: Simon & Schuster, 2003, p. 192.

Page 11, line 23: Ibid., p. 192

Chapter 2
Page 15, line 5: Ibid., p. 16.

Chapter 3
Page 28, sidebar: Samuel Eliot Morison. *John Paul Jones: A Sailor's Biography*. Boston: Little, Brown, and Company 1959, p. 278.

Chapter 4
Page 37, line 15: Ibid., p. 34.

Page 42, line 10: *John Paul Jones: A Sailor's Biography* (Morison), pp. 58–59.

Page 44, line 11: Ibid., p. 91.

Page 45, line 11: Ibid., p. 92.

Chapter 5
Page 48, line 3: *John Paul Jones: Sailor, Hero, Father of the American Navy* (Thomas), p. 120.

Page 48, line 25: Ibid., p. 123.

Chapter 6
Page 55, line 8: Ibid., p. 135.

Page 56, line 16: Ibid., p. 143.

Page 60, line 10: Ibid., p. 174.

Page 60, line 23: Ibid., p. 174.

Chapter 7
Page 66, line 22: Ibid., p. 229.

Page 69, line 25: Ibid., p. 191.

Page 70, line 10: Ibid., p. 192.

Page 72, line 4: Ibid., p. 194.

Chapter 8
Page 78, line 5: Ibid., p. 225.
Page 79, line 19: Ibid., p. 228.
Page 80, line 7: Ibid., p. 228.

Chapter 9
Page 84, line 1: Ibid., p. 244.
Page 84, line 16: Ibid., p. 257.
Page 87, line 9: Ibid., p. 7.
Page 89, line 13: Ibid., p. 283.

Chapter 10
Page 95, line 15: Ibid., p. 4.

Brands, H. W. *The First American: The Life and Times of Benjamin Franklin.* New York: Doubleday, 2000.

Coakley, Robert, and Stetson Conn. *The War of the American Revolution.* Washington, D.C.: Center of Military History, United States Army, 1975.

Cook, Fred. *Privateers of Seventy-Six.* Indianapolis, Ind.: Bobbs-Merrill Company, 1976.

Keegan, John. *The Price of Admiralty: The Evolution of Naval Warfare.* New York: Penguin, 1990.

Lorenz, Lincoln. *John Paul Jones: Fighter for Freedom and Glory.* Annapolis, Md.: United States Naval Institute, 1943.

Morison, Samuel Eliot. *John Paul Jones. A Sailor's Biography.* Boston: Little, Brown, and Company, 1959.

Sobel, Dava. *Longitude.* New York: Penguin, 1995.

Thomas, Evan. *John Paul Jones: Sailor, Hero, Father of the American Navy.* New York: Simon and Schuster, 2003.

Brenda Haugen is the author and editor of many books, most of them for children. A graduate of the University of North Dakota in Grand Forks, Brenda lives in North Dakota with her family.

Image Credits